PURITY

PURITY

By:

Fr Tadros Y. Malaty

ST SHENOUDA PRESS
SYDNEY, AUSTRALIA
2023

Purity
By: Fr Tadros Y. Malaty

COPYRIGHT ©2023
St. Shenouda Press

All rights reserved. Except for brief quotations in critical publications or reviews, no part of this book may be reproduced in any manner without prior written permission from the publisher.

ST SHENOUDA PRESS
8419 Putty Rd,
Putty, NSW, 2330
Sydney, Australia

www.stshenoudapress.com

ISBN 13: 978-0-6451394-4-0

All scripture quotations, unless otherwise indicated, are taken from the New King James Version®. Copyright © 1982 by Thomas Nelson, Inc. Used by permission. All rights reserved.

Contents

What Is Purity?

PURITY AND THE LIKENESS TO CHRIST

'For this is the will of God, Your sanctification: that you should abstain from sexual immorality... Therefore he who rejects this does not reject man, but God, Who has also given us His Holy Spirit.' 1 Thessalonians 4:3,8

The Oxford dictionary defines 'purity' as 'the state of being clean, without evil or sin; unmixed with any other substance or thing/race.'

1 Thessalonians 4:3,8 helps us in formulating a definition for purity. The first is that 'For this is the will of God, your sanctification: that you should abstain from sexual immorality,' and the second, 'Therefore he who rejects this does not reject man, but God, who has also given us His Holy Spirit.'

One may ask:

1. Why does God will our sanctification?
2. Why is rejecting purity considered a rejection of God Himself and not just man?
3. Why is God so interested in our purity?
4. Why does God restrict our freedom? What is the advantage of leading a saintly life?

A simple anecdote will help explain why God is concerned with His children's purity.

When a mother first gives birth to a child, the doctor may comment on how much the child resembles his mother.

At this point, the father of the child may wish that the child look like him. It is here that a paternal contest begins, each wishing the child to resemble themselves. These same feelings of paternal love are the shadow of God's paternal love, in a way that a parent longs to see their children a picture of them through focusing their morals and values. This comes out of intimacy between child and parent; a result of pure, true mutual love with no contradiction of free will. For it is love that makes a father's will one with their son's will, and unites God and man's will. As a result, the children of God should mirror His image – not only by being noble and gentle, but by becoming temples where the Holy Spirit dwells.

Since the fall of Adam, the image of man that carried the likeness of God was distorted. However, the New Adam, Jesus Christ our Saviour, restored the image once damaged by man, and created a new form of practicing the adoption to the heavenly Father.

In the epistle of St Paul to the Ephesians, he emphasises our new nature as the children of God, through which we become the temple of God where the Holy Spirit dwells in our hearts, 'For we are His workmanship, created in Christ Jesus for good works, which God prepared beforehand that we should walk in them.' (Ephesians 2:10)

'Now, therefore, you are no longer strangers and foreigners, but fellow citizens with the saints and members of the household of God, having been built on the foundation of the apostles and prophets, Jesus Christ Himself being the chief cornerstone...in whom you also are being built together for a dwelling place of God in the Spirit.' (Ephesians 2:19-22)

'... till we all come to ... a perfect man, to the measure of Christ;...' (Ephesians 4:13)

These concepts create the core of St Paul's theology. If Saul (St Paul), was questioned about his religious status during the time he persecuted the church, he would have answered, 'I am a righteous man – I know the law, I memorise the prophecies of the Old Testament, I practice fasting, I am a true zealot, a brilliant pioneer and scholar.' When St Paul met the risen Jesus Christ, he discovered that he was on the opposite path completely, before experiencing a yearning to be reunited with God and practice adoption to Him; to be in the likeness of Jesus Christ.

If a believer feels weak or overpowered in his battle against lusts, he needs to dis-cover that he is a child of God. If he stands by himself in the battle of chastity he will be conquered, but it is through God's Spirit that he obtains victory. Once a person discovers his adoption to God, he repents and changes his path through divine grace. Then he discovers that chastity is the natural law of his life. If one ignores their identity as a child of God and a member of the body of Jesus Christ, then sexual immorality becomes the law of his nature. In other words, purity or chastity for a Christian does not belong to the individual, rather they belong to the One who died on the Cross and sent His Holy Spirit to sanctify the church and each member of it.

Let us Begin on a Sound Basis

Lord Jesus, let me know myself and know You,

And desire nothing save only You.

Let me hate myself and love You.

Let me do everything for the sake of You.

Let me humble myself and exalt You.

Let me think of nothing except You.

Let me die to myself and live in You.

Let me accept whatever happens as from You.

Let me banish self and follow You,

And ever desire to follow You.

Let me fly from myself and take refuge in You,

That I may deserve to be defended by You.

Let me fear for myself, let me fear You,

And let me be among those who are chosen by You.

Let me distrust myself and put my trust in You.

Let me be willing to obey for the sake of You.

Let me cling to nothing save only to You,

And let me be poor because of You.

Look upon me, that I may love You.

Call me that I may see You,

And for ever enjoy You.

Amen. Saint Augustine

This is the prayer of Saint Augustine, who was once a proud, blasphemous, perverse young man. Before finding Christ, his father compelled him to get involved in evil deeds, including fornication. In his book 'Confessions,' he admits to having been a leader of a 'gang' that would steal neighbours' apples and feed them to the pigs. St Augustine did not wish to eat the fruit, but merely to fulfil his desire of stealing with the members of his gang as their leader. He even lived in a de facto relationship for twelve years with his illegal wife. It is said that each day, St Augustine would pray to God, asking that He would allow him to repent and live a true life of chastity and purity, 'Give me chastity and continency, only not yet' as he wished to 'satisfy' his needs, rather than 'extinguish' them. One day, he heard of St Anthony the Great. He wondered how a simple Coptic man with no qualifications could be such a great pioneer of the life of monasticism, attracting men to the kingdom of God, while he as a philosopher could not live in chastity and purity. Consequently, St Augustine knelt under a tree and repented.

After seeing him weep fervently, his friend Alypius also repented. The adulterous woman who used to come to him was impressed by the way his life had completely changed. It is said that she knocked on his door and when he asked who she wanted, she replied in wonder, 'Augustine!'

He said, 'Augustine has died.'

She replied, 'It is Augustine's voice!' to which he added, 'Augustine died, Christ is speaking through him!'

She repented and became a Mother Superior, while he became a great saint and a righteous bishop, who drew thousands towards our Lord Jesus.

Saint Augustine knew how to start; that was the secret of his success.

For this reason, our tender mother - the Church - unceasingly teaches us to pray each day saying, 'Let us begin on a sound basis.'

Many who have started and have become bishops, priests, monks and servants to the Church and its congregation, seem to have the mannerisms, zeal and righteousness which are indispensable for worship and evangelization. Nevertheless, in a single moment, they could fall – and, indeed, great could be their fall - because their beginning was not sound.

WHAT IS THE WAY?

How numerous are the short, wide, paths! However, they do not lead to life.

As a youth, you could be attracted to the path of virtue, or to the love of behavioural traits. You may even lean towards a life of service, which could lead you to serving in Sunday School, or to managing the funds earmarked for the poor - both avenues would seem to satisfy the desire of establishing a good relationship with God. Religious fanaticism might even seem to some as the way to devout worship.

My friend, none of the above represents the beginning, the middle, or the end of the path! The path is Encountering our Lord Jesus.

Jesus is the Way, the Truth, and the Life.

If you happen to be agonizing under a sexual or emotional yoke, which is impeding your attempts to fast, pray, or serve, then your first priority is to know our Lord Jesus.

Are you thirsting for a particular sin which you fancy - which could be sexual indulgence or a desire to accumulate wealth? Remember, our Lord Jesus alone is the Paradise of your soul. He is your soul's Bread and Water (John 6:35), your soul's Shepherd and Life (John 10:11), and your soul's Friend and Groom (John 11:25).

Our Lord Jesus is beautiful and sweet. You cannot know Him unless you experience Him. If you do not know Him, you are incapable of loving Him. If you are unable to love Him, then how can you live with Him and through Him? For this reason, cry to Him openly, 'O Lord, reveal Yourself unto me. I desire to know You, since I wish to love You!' In your pleading cries to Him, never assume that He is outside you or distant from you. Rather, He is within you, and closer to you than your own soul.

If you seek to experience our Lord Jesus, pour out your heart candidly to Him, saying, 'My Lord, I desire to love You, even though I do not wish to sacrifice anything for the sake of Your love. I choose to read erotic stories over Your Book, I delight in the company of evildoers while I drag my feet to stand before You, I prefer to visit others than be in Your house. My Lord, enable me to love You.'

Augustine was frank - he repeated similar and stronger words, and the Lord did not abandon him.

DISCOVER YOUR ABILITIES AND GIFTS!

My God, since without You nothing would have been created, then being away from You makes us nothing, through sin.

Woe is me! Darkness has prevailed over me and, although You are the Light, I have hidden my face from You.

Woe to me! My wounds are many and, although You are the Comforter granting peace, I have distanced myself from You.

Woe to me! I have committed a multitude of follies and, although You are the Truth, I have never sought Your counsel.

Woe to me! I have strayed down numerous paths and, although You are the Way, I have separated myself from You.

Woe to me! I have suffered numerous strikes from death and, although You are the Life, I was never with You.

Woe to me! I often fall into evil and nothingness and, although You are the Word through Whom everything came into being, and without You I would not exist, I have detached myself from You.

Saint Augustine

That was the extent of Augustine's capabilities during his days of wickedness. He was nothing, and he carried the burden of corruption of his heart, mind, instincts, senses, and body - all of which were enveloped by sin, which caused him to deliriously reject any substitute for material pleasures.

It is true that - as he confessed - he felt a tendency to transcend above the animalistic life which he led. However, he had a significant obstacle; namely, the impossibility to lead a chaste life.

He was able to overcome that obstacle only by experiencing our Lord Jesus and accepting His grace.

Therefore, the lax young man who succumbed to the ecstasy of carnal desires cries from his depths saying that he wishes to be pure. But how can he abandon the pleasure that embodied his entire life and being?

He was struggling to listen to the quiet voice yearning to embrace the angelic life, being reluctant to forsake the powerful feelings of pleasure enslaving his person and emotions.

The secret behind this struggle lay in his inability to understand the reality of chastity, coupled with his ignorance of the means at his disposal.

Let us start first with the 'sexual instinct.'

According to some people, 'chastity' could be any of the following:

• Refraining from committing adultery,

- Avoiding any habit or activity which might induce sexual arousals or fulfillment,
- Shielding the eyes from observing something which might give rise to lusts,
- Preventing the senses from being exposed to evil sexual feelings or emotions,
- Avoiding people, places or situations which might stimulate bad pleasure, or
- Shielding the heart from unclean thoughts and from bad emotions or feelings involving the other sex.

The above represent avoidant aspects of chastity; whoever fails in any of these will conclude that chastity is an insurmountable obstacle, or an elusive, imaginary, lifestyle.

Many were crushed in their struggle because of such a perception, as they lost the true, sweet taste of chastity. Therefore today, we need to understand the positive meaning of chastity for us to live and experience it.

Chastity in the Positive Sense

Chastity is the adherence of a person to God alone as the Groom of their soul. It is both the correct understanding of the capability which God granted us, and using it as intended. It is loving and cherishing the heavenly Groom - the soul cleaves to God, while loving and cherishing Him through His grace. The soul thus offers God, through the Holy Spirit, the heart with all its emotions and reactions, the mind with all its imaginations, and the senses with all its feelings. Simply, each member of the body leaps towards the Lord and is consecrated to Him.

Chastity does not constitute inhibition or suppression of those emotions, feelings, or instincts which God created in man, rather it is a powerful leap taken by all of those towards their proper place and intent.

BETWEEN THE CHILD'S IMPOTENCE AND THE YOUTH'S STRUGGLE

Because of their sexual inactivity, neither a young child nor a sexually impotent youth is considered to be leading a chaste life in the true sense of the word. This is the chastity of impotence, rather than the fruit of struggle. On the other hand, if a youth struggling to absorb and respond to the love of God were to stumble and fall, such a setback should in no way be an indication of their defilement or lack of chastity. Chastity is not just 'not falling' - rather, it is loving God, abhorring sin, and fighting it unto death.

Though one may fall seven times, the upright will stand, not by being lazy or frivolous, rather, through their constant struggle and prayer, and a yearning for chastity.

The youth who is fighting the old man – the lust of the flesh - in addition to all the worldly allures and the war with the demon of adultery, should arm themselves with the grace of God, while persevering in their struggle through prayer, confession and partaking of the holy sacraments, with tears, cries, groaning, and strict self-discipline. In this case, even if they were repeatedly tormented by thoughts, leading to a fall, they would be meritorious of the crown of chastity - the chastity of struggle and triumph, not that of impotence.

HOLY INSTINCTS

It is fair to say that those to whom God has granted strong sexual instincts, sensitive emotions, and delicate feelings, are the most vulnerable to fall into sin. It is equally fair to say that if they submitted all their feelings and emotions to the Holy Spirit, they would interact most favourably with God's love, and be envied by all.

Do not be ashamed or envy others if your sexual drive happens to be stronger than that of others. This strong instinct is a gift from God, since '...those members of the body which we think to be less honourable, on these we bestow greater honour; and our unpresentable parts have greater modesty.' (1 Corinthians 12:23)

As well as this, do not despair if you find yourself to be an emotional person. Emotions are a gift from God that help us to live in Christ. If you are not an emotional person, you cannot love God, nor His creation.

Purity does not mean a destruction of our senses and emotions given by God, but their sanctification, as our sanctification is the will of God.

Everything in your body has been created by God, fully pure and undefiled, for we are God's creation. He is the Good Shepherd who creates us good.

CHASTITY FOR ALL

Chastity is neither restricted to one class of people over another, nor should it be attributed solely to hermits and monks. Virtuous married couples and struggling youth may also lay a claim to it - it is a lifestyle available to all. The young man struggling to sanctify his desires will experience it when seeking the strong helping hand of God to rescue him. Similarly, the virtuous husband will have the same experience in having our Lord Jesus as the only Groom of his soul, seeing in his bride a pure holy vessel - not simply an object to temporarily satisfy his desires. His bride is his partner in their unity with the Lord's holy body. The monk's experience will render him drunk with the life of Divine love.

Practical Steps to a Life of Purity

How can I acquire a life of purity, given that I am a youth with sexual instincts, living in a society filled with rousing attractions, and having friends who never cease to incite me to do evil, and who scoff at me if I refrain?

The following clarifications are a prerequisite for answering this question:

1. Never lose sight of the fact that our Lord Jesus' concern with respect to my purity is greater than mine. This is not only because I am the dwelling place of His Holy Spirit, but also because He alone, the Holy One, is able to sanctify me, along with my instincts, emotions, feelings, and every member of my body. This is regardless of the extent of my uncleanness and the degree of evil to which I have sunk.

2. God desires to sanctify me and to retain me as His pure bride. I can only profit from this fact if I interact positively with His work in me, since '...the kingdom of heaven suffers violence, and the violent take it by force.' (Matthew 11:12)

Let us now return to the question; Where do I stand as a youth overtaken by evil, and yearning to lead a life of purity compatible with God's work in me?

FIRST: SANCTIFYING THE THOUGHTS

Acquiring holy thoughts can be difficult. Even attempts aimed at merely getting rid of evil unclean thoughts are challenging. They can sometimes creep inside one's consciousness without realising, or seemingly stem from within oneself, controlling them in their sleep, periods of relaxation, and even while fully awake or working.

To combat this, the following 5 points can assist in sanctifying the thoughts:

1. Never give up.

As long as you are in this body, unclean thoughts will always haunt you. The spirit and the flesh will constantly pull you in opposite directions - each desiring what the other abhors. A child of God, on the other hand, whose resolve is to march in the path of Christ, will reject such thoughts and will not yield to them; rather, they will chase them out immediately and will not attempt to entertain any of them.

The safest avenue is, therefore, to flee. This is corroborated by St Paul the Apostle in his second letter to his disciple Timothy, 'Flee also youthful lusts...' (2 Timothy 2:22) Yielding to these thoughts, even for a few minutes, will require a greater effort to get rid of them and day after day, they will establish roots in your heart and you will have given them control over your life. This is analogous to an unwelcome guest; it is difficult to get them to leave once they have entered.

If you are now at the latter stage, and evil thoughts are controlling you, do not despair. Above all, do not complicate matters by willingly accepting new ideas. You must be courageous in resisting those controlling thoughts, knowing that our Holy God sees your humility, accepts you, and keeps count of each small sacrifice you make in the struggle of maintaining the purity of your thoughts. This is God's intent for you; to retain your sanctity and to refrain from adultery.

It may be useful to train oneself, initially, to the notion that sudden death and Judgment are imminent. This is because the principle of 'love' might not be attractive to a frivolous person. Fear mixed with trust might be a viable starting point; experiencing love will follow.

2. Lustful thoughts may not be the beginning

We must also know that lustful thoughts may not necessarily be the starting point, rather, these thoughts usually take a deceitful form at the outset. For example, a person may yield to daydreaming for long periods of time, dreaming of what may seem to be benign prospects, but which often stray from reality, and lead the dreamer insidiously down the path of fantasy mixed with lustful thinking.

3. Anxiety and lack of dependence on God can lead to unclean thoughts

One factor contributing to unclean thoughts is anxiety coupled with lack of dependence on God. For this reason, many students complain of domination by unclean thoughts during examination periods - their busiest time of year. In their anxiety, they try to escape from reality by resorting to unclean thoughts. A strong remedy against such thoughts is prayer, so that the Lord may grant you peace, internal joy, and reliance on Him. In the book of Leviticus, we learn the laws and rituals of sanctification through sacrificial blood, as that of Jesus Christ, besides several laws around cleansing rituals of the body and tabernacles. This aligns with the aim of our sanctification, which is explicitly declared, '...you shall be holy; for I am holy.' (Leviticus 11:44) It is not only a commandment, but also a promise. When lustful thoughts are attacking you, raise your heart to your heavenly Father, the Holy God, asking Him to fulfil His divine promises.

4. 'Satan establishes his lab in the lazy mind.'

Normally, our minds are active. They may work to build or to destroy, working for good or for evil. The mind does not rest by ceasing to function since, by nature, the thought process cannot stop or 'take a break.' Rather, at times of physical inactivity or sleep, the mind regurgitates what it has reaped during the person's daily activities.

Therefore, the youth who spends much of their time in enjoyment, in merrymaking, in the company of scoffers and in places offering eroticism should not expect their thoughts to be holy during their sleep, or during their times of rest, when their willpower is at its weakest. Conversely, one who uses their time to offer for themselves spiritual food, sincerely and from the bottom of their heart, should expect holy thoughts during those periods of relaxation. Therefore, readings scripture and spiritual books, such as the lives of the saints and their sayings, coupled with memorising and reciting the psalms, are all very helpful in terms of storing for yourself clean thoughts which will satisfy you when you hunger.

5. Use the church's tools to sanctify the mind

The last point to bear in mind pertains to learning and chanting church hymns, spiritual songs, and psalms. These direct the mind towards sanctification, and a close encounter with our Lord Jesus.

May the Lord grant us pure and holy thoughts, focused on our Lord Jesus, and despising all the past, old ones. God be with you.

SECOND: SANCTIFYING THE SENSES

My dear brother... who has fervently sought to be in God and to contact this Holy One Who knows no sin. I beseech you to hearken lovingly unto me and to forgive my weakness.

Control your senses, my dear brother, and be mindful of them - through them death creeps into the unwary person's body...

Direct your sight towards God, thus shielding it from contemplating man's perishing beauty.

Listen to the Almighty's mysteries, in order to protect your ears from listening to all that is disagreeable.

Beware of evil odours - seek, instead, Christ's sweet-smelling aroma.

Preserve your lips - let complete caution fully guard your mouth - let your speech be with God, the Creator.

As for the final sense, that of touch, submit it to the ever-watchful Preserver, seeking chastity in all your actions, in order for the Lord to keep you from evil thoughts.

All those aspiring to preserve themselves and their conscience from evil deeds: let them keep those senses, and submit them into the hands of our trusted God, Who aids the weak.' ' ' The Spiritual Sage, ' St John Saba

God granted you senses, without which you lose your liveliness as a sensitive, feeling human being.

Your senses distinguish you from any other earthly being, since God assigned you a will which plays a significant role in directing your senses.

You may choose to give free rein to those five senses, thereby allowing their strong energy to propel you towards enjoying fellowship with the Lord. On the other hand, you can also succumb to the forces drawing you to the depths of defilement, leading you to wallow in uncleanness, and from there, to your belief that purity does not belong to humans endowed with such senses.

I assure you that, as a youth undergoing difficulties associated with sexual desires, and having no willpower to control all your senses, know that the problem does not lie with the existence of those senses, rather, with directing them and using them to work in their intended function.

But, you say, 'how can I direct my senses to work for good, while my entire life is aflame with lust?'

I am neither demanding that you immobilize your senses, nor suppress their function. On the contrary, I would like you to give them free rein to their maximum possible extent - but only after you have been sanctified internally which, in turn, sanctifies your senses, allowing them to lead you towards spiritual growth. The Holy Spirit is the One Who sanctifies the senses, and He is the One Who is not only close to you but indwells you.

Therefore, you need to interact with the Holy Spirit through fervent and open prayer, asking that He fill your heart and that He enlighten your senses. Our Church has thus taught us to pray daily during the Third Canonical Hour saying, 'O Good Lord, do not take Your Holy Spirit away from us, this which You sent upon Your holy disciples and honourable apostles at the third hour.'

As St Anthony the Great details in his first letter, the Holy Spirit helps us follow the commandments which we have learned. He guides us towards ridding ourselves of lusts, those which stem from the soul independently from the body, and those which are inflicted on the soul through the body.

St Anthony goes on to emphasise how the Holy Spirit teaches man to keep his entire body in harmony - from the top of his head to the sole of his feet.

He maintains purity of sight for the eyes, the peaceful listening of the ears, and the refraining of the lips from gossip or slander.

He ensures that the tongue only utters that which is good and well-balanced. He thus does not allow any foul or inappropriate language to be spoken.

He maintains natural movement of the hands, so they may be raised for prayer and for rendering mercy and honour.

He maintains the stomach such that it has suitable limits for food and drink, ensuring that eating is in accordance with the body's needs, thus preventing gluttony.

He keeps the feet along the path of God's will, aiming to perform good deeds.

In this way, the entire body becomes attuned to righteousness, and submits to the authority of the Holy Spirit. The body changes gradually until it finally shares - to a certain extent - the attributes of the spiritual body of Judgment Day.

Spiritual exercise

Memorize the various pieces of the Third Canonical Hour, and recite them fervently, inaudibly, especially in idle times throughout the day.

THIRD: THE STRUGGLE ASSOCIATED WITH SANCTIFYING THE SENSES

Although sanctification is done by the Holy Spirit, the letter of St Anthony also states, 'The struggle to acquire full purity requires, in matters of repentance, that both body and soul fight together, equally and harmoniously.' Furthermore, St Paul says in this regard, 'But now in Christ Jesus you who once were far off have been brought near by the blood of Christ.' (Ephesians 2:13)

The Holy Spirit will only work within us to the extent of our interaction with Him, through hard work and struggle. As mentioned previously, the first step in a life of struggle is prayer, coupled with the quest for a life continually filled with the Spirit, and a constant effort to keep the senses away from any potential source of offence. This will lead us to move towards all that is holy in the sight of the Lord, being filled with His grace.

Let us now look at the struggle associated with each of the senses:

1. The sense of sight

St Augustine considers this to be the first element in a person's downfall. Here are some practical things to do when feeling tempted by the sense of sight:

a) Flee the place where you might feel weaker around a particular person. The reason may not necessarily be that person, rather, your own internal weakness. Such an escape would be attributed to courage, not cowardice, since you will have succeeded in resisting a strong emotion within you. You should, however, not content yourself with this negative action; rather, continue with repentance (returning to God), prayer, and enjoying Jesus your Saviour, looking forward to having innocent eyes which are not susceptible to being offended by anyone.

b) Let not your eyes wander, seeking erotic scenes. Remember that David, the Psalmist, fell into sin through one careless glance.

c) Do not regard others searchingly, seeking sexual arousal; rather, remember that you should regard those before you as family members towards whom you have no sexual tendencies.

d) Do not trick yourself into believing that you are simply contemplating the person's beauty for beauty's sake, since beauty represents the absolute 'good'. Beware of the disguised desire lurking behind it.

e) If you feel you are looking at someone 'abnormally', in any given circumstance, lift your heart to God crying, 'The Name of Jesus!' This will sanctify your sight.

f) Make sure to hang images of our Lord Christ and the saints in your room and on your desk to remember the sanctity of Whom they portray, and the purity of their lives.

g) Stay away from bad sites, books, magazines, and movies which depict romantic and inappropriate erotic scenes. Know that your time is much more precious than to be wasted on such nonsense.

2. The sense of hearing

a) Where practical, flee the company of scoffers. This protects your ears from obscene, lascivious, or erotic talking, jokes and anecdotes. Fleeing will save you from having these thoughts return to your mind at times of relaxation, such as during daydreaming, sleep, extreme fatigue, or sickness.

b) If you like to listen to music, know full well that many have entered the depths of fellowship with God through the beautiful church hymns, especially those sung during Passion Week. These can satisfy your hobby while benefitting your soul.

3. The sense of taste

a) Make sure that your food intake is well suited to your health and to your physical activities.

4. The sense of smell

a) Remember that you should not indulge in adornment and worldly appearances. Your preference should be a life of watchfulness and prayer, that would qualify you to be a source of Christ's sweet-smelling aroma for those who are saved.

5. The sense of touch

a) Ensure, especially in crowded places, that your heart is raised to the Lord; that you call upon His name, and that your mind is focused on Him.

Finally, may the Lord grant us the knowledge that all our members and senses are the Lord's. Remember that you are a child of God; that you have been redeemed by His Son's precious blood, and that He holds you in high esteem. Keeping this in mind, you will then have no difficulty in directing all your energy to work in full accord with the will of God.

The Incarnate God & the Life of Purity

Glory be to You... Who have adopted Adam's perishable body and converted it to a source of life to the perishing.

You have descended from on high to the lowly, to hand out to them Your treasures.

Glory to Him, Who took from us in order to give us; we take from Him, in great abundance, that which is His, through that which is ours.

Indeed, through this 'intermediary' humanity has acquired life through its Helper.

You have found Yourself a body, and became as a slave, in order to offer us that which is acceptable to You, and that which gladdens us. St Ephraim the Syrian

Let us now have a closer look at the body from which you are suffering, echoed by St Paul, 'O wretched man that I am! Who will deliver me from this body of death?' (Romans 7:24) This discussion follows our preceding arguments concerning our misuse of God's gifts of 'thought and senses,' which He granted us to help us enjoy our fellowship with Him.

YOUR BODY IS A GIFT FROM GOD

This very body from which you are suffering, asserting that nothing good dwells therein (Romans 7:18), is a beautiful gift offered to you from the Creator Who loves you and Who desires your well-being. But why then did this body become a gateway to sin?

Adam disobeyed his God; consequently, his body disobeys his soul, even though the soul may reject uncleanness, and yearn for a life of purity.

So, what is the solution?

God, Who loves you, did not seize from you the body which continues to bother your soul. Rather, He sent His Only Begotten Son - the Creator - in the same body which you have. He came from a sinful pedigree and was counted among the transgressors. He came 'in the likeness of sinful flesh" (Romans 8:3) while He, Himself, was sinless.

He came forward and struggled for your sake to offer you triumph in your body, if you put on our Lord Jesus, unite with Him, and interact with His work.

Through His fasting and seclusion, our Lord Jesus intended to heal us from lust's attraction. Thus, for the sake of us all, He accepted to be tempted by Satan, in order for us to learn how to triumph in this body. St Ambrose

Christ triumphed over Satan and crowned human nature with the crown of glory and victory. St Cyril the Great

PRACTICAL STEPS TO PURIFYING THE BODY

1) Transposing the preceding discussion into the practical realm, we can say that our Saviour Jesus did not fast for us not to fast anymore, rather, in order for us to fast in Him. Put differently, fasting alone, without tying it to the fasting Christ, has no value other than subjecting the body and suppressing

its senses. This will lead to rebellion and distress, and any resulting effects will disappear as soon as the fasting period ends.

Let your fast, therefore, be tied to Jesus your Saviour. Do not restrain your voice, since He desires that you call on Him and that He call on you. Cry to Him, and reproach Him whenever you suffer from lustful feelings or thoughts. Train yourself to cry out saying, 'My Lord Jesus Christ, have mercy on me!' everywhere and as often as you can. Set aside for yourself 'quiet times' wherein you meditate on the Person of our Lord Jesus, on His love, on His passion, on His suffering for you, and on the inheritance awaiting you. You will quickly feel, on your own, the heavy yoke imposed on your body by those unclean thoughts, and you will spontaneously say, 'For the good that I will to do, I do not do; but the evil that I will not to do, that I practice.' (Romans 7:19)

2. Fasting does not only mean abstaining from food; rather, say with the apostle: 'I discipline my body and bring it into subjection...' (1 Corinthians 9:27) Subjection means that the body becomes an obedient slave serving its master. Let this body and all its members become enslaved to the will of the Holy Spirit, obeying all the divine commandments.

Your hands, eyes and all other members of your body are Christ's. 'Shall I then take the members of Christ and make them members of a harlot? Certainly not!' (1 Corinthians 6:15)

The benefit is that the body will no longer be a heavy burden on the soul once the person is with our Lord Jesus. Rather, his hands will be raised in prayer, resulting in the soul praying, and in the spirit prostrating itself before its Creator, and rejoicing, as the tongue chants.

My friend, there is no middle ground: your body is either Christ's or Satan's.

3. Do not claim rights for your body, and do not follow the adage, 'Give an hour to the Lord, and let your heart enjoy the next one.' Nothing stands to heal the ailing of your body better than having your soul in full fellowship with Him. It is true the body needs necessities, but I assure you that, on the other hand, your body will rejoice in the soul's happiness, since this is the body's gateway to submission to the Lord.

4. Let your fasting be accompanied by repentance and communion from the Lord's body and blood. This will edify you in Him, and Him in you, as through Him, you will acquire peace, joy, and triumph.

5. Do not transform the celebrations of the feasts into a springboard for the body to indulge in gluttony. The feast does not consist of food and drink; rather, joy and exultation in the Lord Who humbled and impoverished Himself for your sake. You will thus retain the purity and chastity which you enjoyed during the fast. Finally, do not trust this body - rather subjugate it always, and keep it under the Lord's control.

May the Lord keep your body and sanctify your members, so that they become a source of blessing and grace, aiding your soul in its enjoyment of all that is heavenly, and its preoccupation with the Groom, the saints' Holy One. Amen.

What is Love?

Our Church, as a wise mother, maintains a constant, frank dialogue with her children concerning all their problems, even if they might be too self-conscious to address such matters openly. The children, in obeying and trusting their mother, are obliged to accept the Church's stance - which stems from Christ's teachings - even though they might dislike what they hear, or it may require some sacrifice on their part.

THE PROBLEM OF LOVE

This problem is one of the most important issues our children face, and which they hear from numerous sources. God willing, I aim to address several related topics, the first one being 'The concept of love.'

THE CONCEPT OF LOVE

One of the Church's tasks is to rectify the cumulative effects of understandings which the world has injected into our minds; for this reason, St Paul says, 'And do not be conformed to this world, but be transformed by the renewing of your mind...' (Romans 12:2)

Many people assign the label 'love' to some social tendencies or natural instincts, particularly those experienced towards the other sex. Even the Holy Bible, speaking to humans in terms they understand, uses similar terminology. However, the Bible makes a clear distinction between true love and other feelings.

ATTRIBUTES OF TRUE LOVE

A loving person puts their beloved ahead of themselves; they give up their life for the sake of their beloved and their happiness. The Lord Jesus has given us a practical lesson in love, '...in that while we were still sinners, Christ died for us' (Romans 5:8). Christ came forward as a silent Lamb. He didn't utter a word. He accepted to bear all our iniquities, and He endured all the blows inflicted on Him for the sake of His beloved. This is the sacrifice which differentiates true love and lustful love.

Let us consider the example of a high school or college young man who thinks, 'I'm in love with a girl. She is suitable for me and I am comfortable with her. She would make a good wife for me.' In his fear of losing her, he proceeds to extract a promise from her to reject all other suitors and wait for him to graduate.

Let me elaborate on this example and clarify its underlying meaning. This young man is lusting after this girl and, because he loves himself, he desires that she become his wife to make him happy and comfortable, even at the risk of not realising her own career prospects, and/or rendering herself unhappy. Lust is not love; it is something emanating from within a person. It is a projection of oneself onto another, and an indication of loving oneself in the other person. Love means to give oneself to others for the glory and progress of others, whereas lust is to count others as instruments for the satisfaction of the ego and attaining bodily desires.

Therefore, this young man should be honest with himself and, rather than saying 'I love her,' say, 'I love myself and she is well-suited to satisfy my emotions, lusts, and heart's desires.'

LOVE IS SELFLESSNESS, LUST IS SELFISHNESS

In the story of Joseph and Potiphar's wife, St John Chrysostom wondered who really loved the other. Potiphar's wife seemed to love Joseph; her heart clung to him, and she hung onto him, until he finally left her his garment. But if you loved someone, would you force them to do something they hate, to the extent that they run away from you naked?

If you loved someone, would you bear false witness against them before the entire household?

In fact, Potiphar's wife despised Joseph, because she told her husband, 'The Hebrew servant whom you brought to us came in to me...' (Genesis 39:17) She had him jailed through her husband's authority.

On the other hand, Joseph who fled from her presence did love her. He spoke to her kindly and never hurt her feelings. When speaking to Potiphar's wife and referring to him, Joseph addressed him as '...my master...,' (Genesis 39:8), as though he were reminding her that he was her slave. He refrained from saying '...your husband...,' to avoid hurting her feelings by implying that she was cheating on her husband.

He did not lambaste her. Rather, he gently reminded her of both her and her husband's graciousness. He neither criticised her before the prisoners, nor did he narrate his story to Pharaoh.

When he was promoted to becoming second only to Pharaoh, he never thought of avenging himself against her, or even reproaching her.

Do you really love someone? Then, let them lead their own life, and do not cause their heart to be occupied by lustful thinking, which would impede their spiritual and intellectual growth. Why do you fear them becoming betrothed to someone else? Again, if your love for them were sincere, you would desire happiness for them, whether you married them or not. The reason one wants someone only for themselves is because they love themselves more than the other person.

But some might ask, if this is love, then why did God create within us sexual instincts? Is there no love between a man and his betrothed, or between two spouses?

Regarding the first question, the sexual instinct, like all other instincts, is a holy gift, which should be used in accordance with God's intended natural use for it. It is not up to us to use this gift, granted by our Holy God, except in its natural application, at the proper time, having been sanctified by the Lord.

Regarding the second question, whether you are a man or a woman, projecting your love for yourself onto the person of your betrothed or spouse is not an indication of real Christian love. The Church does recognise marital love, but there is a difference between marital love and lustful love. Each member of a loving couple will sacrifice for the other's sake. Even in sexual relations, each of the two spouses will seek to satisfy the other in accordance with the Lord's will, not with the intent of satisfying one's own desires at the expense of the other.

The preceding brief account of the meaning of 'marital love,' is undoubtedly quite different from the notion of a young man meeting a young girl and feeling attracted to her demeanour or her physical beauty, through which he might conclude that she would be an ideal wife satisfying his heart's desires.

LOVE IS LIFE

A self-centred person who is constantly seeking to satisfy his body's desires and tendencies will have uninhibited, misguided, roaming eyes, whose only feedback to him will be that he indeed is in love.

Unless our hearts are opened and filled with the Spirit of God Who indwells us, we will be unable to shed our self-centredness and expend all our energy for the sake of our loved one. To love someone sincerely, be it spouse, offspring, relative, or anybody else, we must surrender our hearts completely to God, who is Love. This, in turn, gives us the true image of Jesus Christ Who gave Himself up for the world.

This is the kind of 'living love' which will guide youth towards full enjoyment of real life, living with an open personality and vibrant, energetic love, devoid of any selfish, concealed desires.

But some might ask; if all love stems from God, and pours into Him, does this mean that man should not consider marriage?

To answer this question, know that a young man living in true love would be active, outgoing, and open to everyone in the Lord after marrying. This person's relationship with his wife would be at a deep spiritual level; he would love her as a part of his body, and as a partner in her membership in the mystery of Christ's body.

He would see beauty in his wife despite others' failure to see it.

He would realise that she is the best suited person for him, since it was God, the bounty giver, Who granted her to him.

He would love his wife, offering her his full emotions in the Lord, without thinking of or considering any other.

He would continue loving his wife no matter what circumstances might befall them. Their physical relationship would be one of the Lord's holy signs, but by no means the only tie between them.

That is the kind of love which edifies the souls of both loving and loved.

As for the physical, lustful, love – it is based entirely on the body and whatever pertains to it (e.g. wit, sense of humour, good taste, wealth, etc.). Such physical love kills the spirit, perturbs the soul, and often leads to weakening the body. This is a deadly love.

For example, Amnon's soul was trapped by the desires of his body. He was enthralled by the beauty of his sister Tamar. The Bible says, 'Amnon was so distressed over his sister Tamar that he became sick; for she was a virgin. And it was improper for Amnon to do anything to her.' (2 Samuel 13:2) Amnon became sick, and his condition worsened every day. Is this not exactly what we hear about many who loved girls or women and whose hearts clung unto them?! They fall ill and might fail in their studies due to their excessive preoccupation with the object of their admiration - not to mention perdition of the very souls for which Christ died!

Amnon managed to satisfy his lust for his sister through trickery, and he subsequently hated her more than he had loved her. He could not stand seeing her, and he kicked her out, despite her bitter pleas that he allow her to stay. His soul, which he had thought abounded with love, was now filled with anxiety, harshness, and cruelty, to the extent that he shut his sister out in great shame.

He inflicted illness and worry on his body and soul, he ruined his sister's psyche, and he wronged his father's household by sowing divisiveness and great shame.

Another example is Samson, the mighty man, who also allowed his soul to be enslaved by the desires of his body. He loved Delilah, succumbed to the lust of his body, and slept on her knees. (Judges 16:19) The end of this mighty man, who had vanquished many, was that he became fettered like a bull to a grinder in prison.

Like them, when Potiphar's wife saw that 'Joseph was handsome in form and appearance' she 'cast longing eyes on Joseph, and she said, 'Lie with me.' (Genesis 39:6-7) When her body blinded her, she forgot all about her social standing, and pleaded with a foreign slave to commit wickedness with her, disregarding the sanctity of her marriage.

These are examples of people who allowed their souls to be blinded by their body's desires. Their spirits perished, their souls suffered, and they even lost their body's aspirations.

Award the first priority to your soul for which Christ died, in order to be dead to terrestrials, and to exult in celestials.

UNCONCEALED LOVE

A living, giving love is unafraid of light. Man proclaims it openly, just as Christ proclaimed His love for all on the Cross. Conversely, when David's heart desired the wife of Uriah the Hittite, he asked for her secretly, but his evil was revealed, since '...there is nothing covered that will not be revealed, nor hidden that will not be known.' (Luke 12:2) Indeed, one can stoop so low as to boast before others of his lustful desires.

This is especially true in the company of a crowd their own age. On the other hand, this person stands to be ashamed of themselves since they have become a submissive slave to the body of a person. The Lord is able to free our hearts from all slavery, so that we may love all in the Lord, through Him and for Him, leading a life in the Spirit.

Spirituality and Withdrawal

Sometimes, when speaking about ridding oneself of lustful love, some youth are led to believe that every one of the opposite sex must be regarded as an evil demon from whom we should flee. This perception, in turn, culminates in their withdrawal from their surroundings and society. In their view, a pious person should isolate themselves completely from everything and everyone.

This is what we have observed in some youth who purport to be pious, and who believe that their piety necessitates isolation from family, relatives, colleagues, and society.

This will often take the form of

a) At home, we find youth living in complete isolation under the guise of 'piety,' having withdrawn from all communication and fellowship with members of their family. They do not share in their troubles, happiness, or hardships, and considers themselves to be the only person who prays, fasts, sacrifices, and meditates on the Holy Bible. They preach this, and despise all deeds of their family members.

b) Whether they be in an academic or business setting, they view all people as being 'evil.' They flee socialising and are completely withdrawn.

c) They live in isolation, as a secluded society within a society. They have no interest in knowing anything about their surrounding community. Strangely enough, when blamed or questioned about their attitude, they consider that criticism to be the cross they have to carry for the Lord. This, in turn, increases their efforts to withdraw. Unfortunately, all of this propels them to be defensive both with others and with themselves.

On the other hand, we have a class of youth that perceives spirituality as being a vibrant lifestyle, unimpeded by rules or plans. They confuse liberty with unruliness and anarchy.

This group believes that freedom means doing what they want, in any way they want, unrestricted and unfettered. They have no problem sitting for hours on end watching erotic shows or movies, and they lack the impetus to get up and pray or study the Holy Bible. This is all done under the label of 'freedom' and under the pretext that worship is done within the heart, with no need for such things as prayer, fasting, studying, etc.

A person in this group would allow themselves to participate in consumption of alcohol and drugs with friends and family members at parties, considering this a part of their freedom. Again under 'freedom,' they might engage in secluded, inappropriate, conversations with the opposite sex, in order not to be accused of being unduly moralistic. Furthermore, they would engage in laughter or depraved conversations having sexual connotations, under the guise of 'embracing everyone.'

Many of our youth stand before those two significantly different groups and wonder:

1. What do we mean, then, by spirituality? What is withdrawal?

2. Why do some pious people resort to withdrawal?

3. To what extent should I be open to others, and interact with them, and when should I opt for withdrawal?

4. To what extent should I associate with the other sex?

May the Lord give us an opportunity to respond to these questions, and others.

CONCEPT OF SPIRITUALITY

'God is Spirit, and those who worship Him must worship in spirit and truth.' (John 4:24) Put differently, they prostrate and worship through God; hence, spirituality is man's attachment and adherence to God Who indwells him.

It is the enjoyment of the Saviour's Person in our lives; our increasing edification in Him, while offering all that is ours to Him.

It is the submission, within God's hands, of our hearts, senses, emotions, members, and all our soul's and body's energies.

It is full surrender to God, instead of, 'Me, Myself and I', it is placing Christ first in all my thoughts, conversations, and conduct.

It is walking along the Lord's path and enjoying His work in us through prayer, fasting and studying the Holy Bible.

It is constant unity with the Lord in our lives, especially through the holy sacraments.

CONCEPT OF WITHDRAWAL

Withdrawal, on the other hand, represents the exact opposite of spirituality; this is because it constitutes the soul's revolving around 'Me, Myself and I'.

For a withdrawn person, worship revolves around himself and not around the Lord. His prayers will not probe the depths of his soul, soaring with it to the Lord's heavenly heights. Rather, he locks himself up within his soul, seeking to submit the Lord to his own self. His prayers therefore only serve to appease his conscience and to elicit praise from others or even from himself. Such a person would not know how to talk candidly to the Lord as His Father. Fasting would only be practiced to satisfy the person's ego. He would talk about himself often, seeking his and others' admiration for his fasting and worship!

Finally, when that person confesses, he would neither be broken-hearted nor contrite before the Holy Spirit; rather, he would have lengthy accounts of his iniquities with his Father in confession, with no hint of regret or repentance. His primary objective is to solicit his confessor's attention and sympathy. He might even go so far as to serve and to evangelise, without knowing how to preach repentance to his own soul. He delights in the appearance of his service, and in everyone's interest in him and his work.

This is a picture of sick piety. It promotes the self, relies on self-righteousness, and the person remains unrepentant. In fact, 'piety' is a misnomer. This is better described as isolationism – isolating the soul from others. The person does not adhere to the Lord as the Lover of Mankind, and therefore sees this as his calling to love everyone. Rather, he withdraws from society, even from God Himself, despite the outward appearance of worship and service. He is engrossed only by material matters related to the service, without the ability to be preoccupied with the Lord.

In this case, the soul and everything else is wrapped around the self.

WHAT IS SPIRITUALITY WITHIN THE CHURCH?

A spiritual person follows in the footsteps of our Lord Jesus. Our Lord Jesus indeed came into this world with principles which the world neither tolerated nor accepted. Despite the fact that this made Him a stranger in this world, He walked among the people as one of them with neither pride, disdain, haughtiness, nor contempt for anyone, no matter how they erred. Our Jesus came for the world's sake, not to condemn the world or be isolated from it. 'For God so loved the world that He gave His Only Begotten Son...' (John 3:16)

Since His childhood, Jesus opened His heart to obey His parents, and He never exalted Himself throughout His service. He conversed with the Samaritan woman, He had pity on a harlot, He opened His heart to an outcast tax collector, and He spoke with the young children. Finally, He spread His arms on the Cross to proclaim His love for all, and to proclaim His desire to serve everyone.

This is the Spirit of our God, and this should be the spirit of all who experience Him: to serve everyone and to be open to everyone with no exception. 'For if you love those who love you, what reward have you?... And if you greet your brethren only, what do you do more than others?... Therefore you shall be perfect, just as your Father in heaven is perfect.' (Matthew 5:46-48)

This is perfection. Our heavenly Father delights in humans. He loves and desires salvation for all. The sun of His blessings rises over all humanity, even over the heretics and those who blaspheme His Name. Similarly, whenever God's children unite with their heavenly Lord, their hearts burn with love for all their fellow humans, as seen in the hermits and those living in isolated monasteries. They isolate themselves in order to be closer to God Who indwells us, whereby their love for humanity should be greater than ours.

We learn these principles from our Church whose loving heart is open to all. During the Divine Liturgy, with our slaughtered Lord before us on the altar, and while the Church is preoccupied with the wondrous sacrifice, she asks the clergy and congregation to pray for the shepherds and flock, the leaders and troops, the elderly and youth, the sick and heavy-laden, the needy and the rich, and even the plants, herbs and wind.

The presence of the sacrifice on the altar opens our hearts to embrace everyone, and to pray for our weakness and for the wellbeing of the entire world. This is not due to any worthiness or righteousness on our part, rather, to the love of Him Who loves the world, and Who gave up His body and blood for all.

Another marvellous facet of our Church's teaching is that even those who have reposed in the Lord continue to pray for us with their open hearts, while we also pray for them, although we may not know their names.

Analogously, each child of Christ and the living Church should be open to loving and serving all, even the enemies and troublemakers.

Such humility, proclaimed by the Lord and revealed by the Church, does not constitute random or haphazard openness. It's clear aim is that the knowledge of truth and the presence in the bosom of God be attained by all for the ultimate enjoyment of eternal life.

The Lord accepted the adulteress, who was caught in the act, and who was sentenced to be stoned to death by the religious community. The same humble Lord strongly rebuked the Pharisees, Sadducees and lawyers – not because they angered Him or desired to kill Him, rather, in order for them to know the truth and return to their senses.

The same love which drove Christ to converse for hours with the Samaritan woman led Him to stand silently before Pilate, to give him a chance to reconsider his position.

Whatever we say about Christ applies to the Church – His bride. Through her love and openness for all, she opens her doors indiscriminately, and lovingly isolates the deceitful for their chastisement and for the protection of her children.

To recap, we can say that our Lord Jesus Christ and His Church open their arms wide for everyone, while ensuring that they do not deviate from the truth, even if this entails driving them to the Cross.

Hence, every true son should be open inwardly to accept salvation, and also open to others, since the Lord died for them, regardless of their origins, religion, habits, mannerisms, and regardless of the extent of their love or absence thereof.

There are others, however, who do frequent church services but, in reality, are quite distant from the Church. Unfortunately, their purpose is just to socialise with a community in isolation from the outside world. This gives them satisfaction in accordance with their perception, and not in accordance with God's will. They mingle with believers in order to hear their praise, while concealing their faults under ostentatious expressions which they themselves do not comprehend, such as spiritual silence, spiritual inclinations to monasticism, spiritual seclusion, etc. In so doing, they fail both in meeting with the loving Lord, and in developing a full understanding of those spiritual meanings in Orthodoxy.

To correct such misconceptions, a person needs to be alert and fully cognizant of their faults and weaknesses, rather than attempting to couch them in misleading expressions. Furthermore, owning up should be done candidly with the person's confessor, at the foot of the Cross, and in the light of the Holy Spirit Who indwells us. The goal is the salvation of that person's soul, not the consolidation of their social standing. The personality will be edified as a natural consequence.

The Church opens her doors hospitably to all. However, unless we submit ourselves to the Holy Spirit at the hands of our father of confession, we will remain enclosed, and our worship will degenerate to blind fanaticism, self-righteousness, and disdain for others. The Church stands for the exact opposite of those principles.

PURITY OF THE INNER MAN

'Do not let your adornment be merely outward—arranging the hair, wearing gold, or putting on fine apparel —rather let it be the hidden person of the heart...' 1 Peter 3:3-4

Purity is not just being clean of lustful actions or even thoughts, but rather purity touches our inner life (the hidden person of the heart). Purity means that we are not absorbed in the outer ornaments, but rather looking at our inner life.

The problem is that we do not consider the inner life to be an actual life, or a practical one. We only understand the outer things which we can sense and are visible to us. However, a human being is not merely a body. Every being has a body and soul, and we cannot separate them except by death. Even after death, the body and soul will reunite whether one is recompensed or eternally punished. Therefore, we should be eager to possess a pure heart and be watchful of our inner being. If we are more concerned with outer appearances, it is easier to be unclean, because we are occupied with what is temporary. However, if we focus on our inner life, it is easier to live in purity.

Through our concern with the inner man, we acknowledge that we are not just mortal creatures, but that our souls are immortal. Some Fathers of the Church say that there are three kinds of deaths:

1. Death to sin,

2. Death to God, and

3. Bodily death.

The soul will not die. It will live eternally, either in eternal life or eternal punishment. The soul will perish if it is separated from the source of its life; God Himself. If we honour and evaluate our souls, it is easy to give up bodily lusts, because we appreciate how precious our souls are.

Our Lord Jesus Christ said, 'The kingdom of God is within you.' (Luke 17:21) The Jews were looking forward to an earthly kingdom, but Christ established His kingdom in our hearts. Therefore, if you want to be pure, look at your inner man and care about the salvation of your soul.

When the two saints Maximus and Dometius, the sons of Emperor Valentinus, were occupied by their inner man, they left their noble life to live in a cave in the desert of Egypt. If one was to ask them of the life which they had left behind in their father's palace, they would say, 'We are now the happiest people in the world.' Therefore, when you look within your heart and truly struggle for the salvation of your inner man, putting your life in the hands of God and responding to the work of the Holy Spirit in your heart, you will be the most joyful person in the world. If this is the case, you will never be conquered by any lusts or defilement, practicing purity in all aspects of your life.

Picture a student who is about to receive their Ph.D., and is on their way to discuss their work in front of professors, students and friends, and he is insulted by a driver. Do you think that this will affect them? They will accept the insult – or, precisely, they won't care – because they are more focused on the degree of excellence they are about to receive. Similarly, as a child of God, if someone insults you, you say, 'my time is too precious to be occupied with this problem,' since you are concerned with the kingdom of God within your heart.

St Paul, who wants us to be absorbed in the inner kingdom, asks us not to enter into useless arguments which do not redeem the time, so that we do not speak idly (Ephesians 4:29 & 2 Timothy 2:23). A person occupied with trivial matters such as answering back will not see the preciousness of their inner life. St Peter gives us the key to purity, 'the hidden person of the heart' (1 Peter 3:4).

Contemplating on the glory of our inner man helps us not only abstain from bodily lusts, but also purity of all sins. For example, a believer who is concerned with the inner glory hates to be hypocritical, saying, 'I am not afraid of being exposed by others, nor afraid of society or even of my own conscience, but rather I am afraid of destroying the kingdom of God which has been established in my heart. How can I deceive others by my sweet words while I am the image of heaven itself?!' If your citizenship is in heaven, then worldly problems become trifles. Therefore, this is the key to our purity – that we lift up our hearts to heaven. As St Augustine says, 'Let your hearts be lifted up, then all the members of your body will be lifted up.' In this way, we can even influence those around us. For example, St Anthony the Great had forsaken all and paid attention to the kingdom of God within him, so that through his life, he was able to bring the heretics back to the church because they saw him caring for his inner man.

The Lasting Effect of Purity

PURITY THAT SHINES INTO EVERY ASPECT OF YOUR LIFE

'I beseech you therefore, brethren, by the mercies of God, that you present your bodies a living sacrifice, holy, acceptable to God, which is your reasonable service. And do not be conformed to this world, but be transformed by the renewing of your mind, that you may prove what is that good and acceptable and perfect will of God.' Romans 12:1-2

I feel happy to use the word 'shines' because when we speak about purity, we may view it as the sun. When Jesus Christ Himself, the Sun of Righteousness and Holiness, shines in our life, granting us to be in His likeness, we also shine on others by His rays of purity.

St Paul says here in verse 1, 'I beseech you therefore, brethren, by the mercies of God, that you present your bodies a living sacrifice, holy, acceptable to God, which is your reasonable service.' What is the relation between purity and self-sacrifice?

As we have discussed in previous chapters, purity is not merely abstaining from sin, but also practicing love, by offering oneself to others and denying one's ego.

St Paul used to sacrifice himself every day, considering a day without a spiritual sacrifice as a lost day; 'But what things were gain to me, these I have counted loss for Christ.' (Philippians 3:7) He knew that he would receive as much as he gave to others for Christ's sake. The same applies to purity. For instance, we may often wonder why we deprive ourselves of pleasures, such as going to certain parties or not watching certain entertainment programs. However, as St Paul experienced, when we sacrifice earthly pleasures, we receive a more precious heavenly reward. Therefore, purity is not only to prevent yourself from worldly pleasures, but to receive the Lord of Righteousness in your heart.

How was it possible for the 18-year-old Isaac to accept to be sacrificed by Abraham, who was more than 110 years old at the time? He saw the sign – together with his father – of the crucified and risen Lord Jesus Christ, and accepted to be sacrificed with Jesus so that he could rise with Him.

Purity changes you from a man into an angel. It is said that a monk once approached Pope Shenouda III when he was a bishop, complaining about the abbot of his monastery and saying that he dealt harshly with him. He asked if he should leave and go to another monastery. Pope Shenouda answered him and said, 'Do not worry about how he deals with you. Start to live in fellowship with Christ, and then all the monks and the abbot will see that you are a man of God and will fear harming you, lest God punishes them.' Therefore, when we have God on our side, through purity, we have the solution to our problems.

A person who was working on a project in Alexandria once came to me and gave a sincere confession. He told me that it was the first time he had ever confessed, even though he was about 30 years old. It was many talks with a 20-year-old relative of his, whom he used to mock as a child, that influenced him to return to God and repent for all the sexual relations he had in the past. After taking holy communion for the first time since his childhood, he returned to me proclaiming God's mercy on him. He told me that some people from the street who abused drugs and were violent towards him had just knocked on his office door, wanting to apologise and become his friends. His attackers became his protectors and his close friends. I realised that when he became reconciled with God, God granted reconciliation with others, even with his enemies. When your heart becomes pure, all the aspects of your life will be totally changed. We must bear in mind how much the blessing of God affects our life.

Purity changes a man into an angel. The person who lives in purity lives in Jesus Christ and has the power of the Holy Spirit working in their heart. On the contrary, the person who insists on sinning, though he may be popular, ultimately suffers from loneliness, because his sins separate him from God. If I am truly pure in Christ, and I am the temple of the Holy Spirit, then even if all people forsake me, I will never feel lonely.

PURITY MAKES YOU A KING!

Joseph, the son of Jacob, had a pure heart. Wherever he went, God blessed him and made him prosper. He was a decent, obedient, pure-hearted person, yet he was sold as a slave, tempted by his master's wife, and sent to jail. Even in jail, the guard respected him and gave him the authority to do as he pleased before he was freed and sat on the throne of Pharaoh of Egypt. Purity granted Joseph to be lifted from his house to jail to the throne, where his whole family lodged in time of famine. Joseph, who was responsible for nourishing people in the critical period of famine, symbolised Jesus Christ who is the nourishment of the whole church through His body and blood. This was the fruit of purity. Although he was sold, he did not feel like a slave within himself, but rather felt inner freedom in Jesus Christ.

In contrast, Ptolemy, one of the kings of Egypt, was a slave to the beauty of Cleopatra, and lost his throne. Although he was mature in the eyes of his people because of his age and position, he could not satisfy his lusts, hence losing his throne and becoming a bad example to the whole world. This is how lust can change a king into a slave!

PURITY CHANGES YOUR LIFE INTO HEAVEN

Purity is Christ Himself who shines in your life, in every aspect of your life; at home, school, work, in your worship, in your relationship with others, in your thoughts – all the aspects of your life can be transformed into heaven when you have purity.

It is said that one day an artist wanted to depict the image of Jesus Christ. He noticed a pleasant, beautiful, and smiling person, whose face declared his inner calm and peace. So, he started drawing his portrait. After several years, he wanted to depict Judas Iscariot, the betrayer. He noticed a grieved person who looked depressed, so he decided to draw his portrait. The person asked the artist, 'Do you remember me?' The artist did not remember him, so he continued, 'I am the same person you drew several years ago.' The artist said 'How? Your face has changed completely!' The person replied, 'Sin!'

Sin has a great effect on your body, on your thoughts, and on your behaviour. It ruins all aspects of your life. On the other hand, purity transforms all aspects of your life.

When we speak of purity, we are speaking about God Himself. Try to experience this - not through books, not through homilies or sermons, but through the true practice of purity. We can conclude by saying that if you want to live as if you are in heaven, live in purity.

Therefore, when St Paul says: 'I beseech you therefore, brethren, by the mercies of God, that you present your bodies a living sacrifice, holy, acceptable to God, which is your reasonable service. And do not be conformed to this world, but be transformed by the renewing of your mind, that you may prove what is that good and acceptable and perfect will of God" (Romans. 12:1-2), he is making a correlation between bodily sacrifice and the renewal of the mind.

PURITY'S EFFECT ON OUR INNER LIFE

When you have purity, you enjoy the harmony of all your abilities. An impure person is in conflict – his spirit and his flesh are contrary to one another (Galatians 5:17). His mind wants to be lifted up to God, while his body is inclined to his lusts. Do not think that the body and mind are at peace when one leads a sinful life, because the natural law within us, which even the non-believers have, is working in the minds and hearts of human beings.

Once, when I was in the church of St Mark in Los Angeles, we were all sitting in the church hall. At around midnight, a young women knocked on the glass and entered. She was Palestinian, and she asked if we spoke Arabic, for she wanted to hear Arabic. I asked of her and of her marital status, and she replied that she wasn't married, but that she had a boyfriend. I asked her how long she had been with her boyfriend. She answered, 'For a few months. I've lived with many boyfriends, some for years and others for months.' Then I asked her, 'Are you happy?' She replied, 'Do you want me to speak frankly? I use drugs. I spend my nights at parties with boyfriends. I may appear to be a happy person, but in my heart, I feel like the most miserable person in the whole world. I'm not sure how I'm alive. I've become a person whose miserable state has led to a corrupt life which I can't leave behind.'

When I spoke to her about God, she refused to accept God as a Father because she didn't taste fatherhood and didn't know what it meant. 'I don't see my father taking care of me, or loving me,' she said. I asked her, 'Where is your father?' She didn't know where he was staying, and likewise her mother. I asked her if she would ask about their parents' health if they were sick. She said, 'No, why should I ask about the health of my father or mother? There are many hospitals and doctors!' She didn't care what happened to her parents. This is the fruit of sin. She was deprived of parental relationship thus lacked the tender feelings of family love. She appeared happy in her popularity with many boyfriends and in going to many parties, but in fact, she was suffering a feeling of loneliness, thinking that nobody cared for her. Hence, she was not ready to care for any person, not even her parents.

Sin isolates us from God, from our humanity, and from those around us. Purity in Jesus Christ, through the work of the Holy Spirit, grants us the experience of unity with God, the reconciliation with our souls, and the harmony of our lives, as well as reconciliation with others.

QUESTIONS & ANSWERS

Q1 How Can We Control Our Emotions So That They Do Not Supercede Our Thoughts?

We should distinguish between 'controlling' our emotions and 'sanctifying' them. 'Controlling' implies restriction. It is important to control our emotions, but not to the same extent as a rider would bridle his horse and thus gain control. It is not merely important to control your emotions but to 'sanctify' them to be directed in the right way.

For example, if someone is riding a chariot and it is heading in the wrong direction or in a dangerous way, a good driver would not stop it, as he would crash. Rather, he would guide it to travel in the right way with wisdom. There are two steps to do this:

a. Leaving what is evil, and

b. Doing what is good.

This is what Prophet David states in his psalms, 'Depart from evil and do good.' (Psalms 34:14) To leave what is evil is not sufficient. You should also do what is good. The two actions work together.

This doesn't mean to have no emotions, but rather controlled ones. At the same time, we ask the Holy Spirit to change our emotions for the edification of the church and for our own spiritual progress.

It is essential to have emotions. A priest without emotions cannot practice tender fatherly love. Anyone who lives with Jesus Christ is not emotionless, rather they have well directed emotions under the guidance of the Holy Spirit. For example, in the liturgy, the priest prays for the sick, travellers, widows, strangers, prisoners, the deceased, and even for rivers and trees. During the liturgy of the Eucharist, the priest expresses his emotions not only towards God, but also towards the heavenly creatures and all the world in Jesus Christ.

An example of this is St John Chrysostom, who had warm feelings towards his people. When he used to leave them for a single day, he declared that he missed them as if it had been a year. He told his people that he loved them more than his eyes, because what was the advantage of having eyes without his beloved people?

Likewise, St Anthony the Great had many children in monasticism to whom he expressed great love. He loved not only his children, but the entire world, and he used to pray for all men. His contemporary, St Paul the Hermit, remained over seventy years in the desert without seeing a single person, yet he was still praying for the whole world. God told St Anthony that because of His beloved Paul's prayers, He had blessed Egypt and the waters of the Nile. Even monks and hermits who lead a rough life in the desert have deep feelings towards all humans through their deep connection to Christ. Thus, they pray for the salvation of the entire world.

Q2 What Is The Meaning Of Perfect Holiness Or Purity?

Perfection is relative. What's perfect for you is imperfect for St Anthony the Great, and what is perfect for him is imperfect for others. Every believer resembles a vessel. Once it is full, he considers himself satisfied. However, the more one spiritually grows, the more he feels imperfect, acknowledging the long journey to reach perfection.

St Paul wanted to be in the likeness of Jesus Christ – 'the measure of the stature of the fullness of Christ' (Ephesians 4:13) – so he strived to grow each day. Thus, he was able to see that although the way was infinite, he need not despair, as every time he attained an element of perfection or purification, this meant he deserved to be crowned. He was persistent in attainting the image of Jesus Christ because he is a member of His body, rejoicing each step of the way. Note however that man cannot attain absolute perfection, which is a character belonging to God alone.

Q3 How Do We Know If We Are Pure?

You can feel it. Here are some examples:

1. When a person sees something or someone beautiful, if they envy this person, or desire to satisfy their own emotions with this beauty, they are impure. If they glorify the Creator, then they are pure, as they are looking to what is beautiful in sanctity.
2. If a person's mind is absorbed in seeking what is earthly, such as looking for the latest fashion clothes, hair style etc., these things are not sins in themselves, but the heart which is absorbed in them is not clean. The true Christian's mind will not be constantly occupied with it.
3. A believer who spends their time working may contemplate on Jesus Christ throughout their day, feeling that they are in the presence of God. Even while doing something simple like gardening, their heart is inflamed for the salvation of all human beings. This is purity which one practices even when working in a garden!

Purity is not only practiced as limiting the body against its lusts, but it involves our entire being. It is a sanctification of all aspects of our life.

Q4 Is It Possible To Contemplate On God Whilst Working When Your Job Requires A Great Deal Of Concentration?

There was a brain surgeon who was a genius. Once, a lady went to him so he could diagnose her symptoms. She had a brain tumour and needed to have an operation to remove it. She asked him about the likely success rate of the operation. He paused, then asked her if she believed in God and prayed to Him. She answered 'Yes.' He continued saying that before he performs any operation, he asks God to grant him success, and it is then up to God to make the decision and to determine the outcome of the operation. He stated that it wasn't her work, nor was it his job, but God's. This surgeon felt that even while he was occupied with such a serious and possibly fatal operation, it was God, not him, Who was working, and the surgeon had performed a great number of operations successfully. Therefore, if you begin your work with a prayer asking God to work with you, and pray even whilst you are working (even for a few seconds), saying, 'God save me, God help me, Christ be with me', you will feel that you are in the presence of God and absorbed in Him whilst you are working.

Q5 *In Today's Society It Is More Enjoyable Or Easier Being Impure. How Can We Have This Desire To Really Love Purity?*

You need to taste the sweetness of purity. Ask God to grant you this experience. Once, a youth came up to me asking, 'Do you believe that any youth is able to live without having a relationship with the other sex. Can one truly live this kind of life, or will it make him depressed?' Initially he thought that when a person lives in purity, he would be depressed as he would be forsaking things that make life enjoyable, such as going to parties, having relations and being happy. After speaking to him about purity, he repented, and found true joy in the life of purity. After tasting and experiencing it, he concluded that purity is life and uncleanliness is death. It is important to practice and examine the sweetness of purity.

Q6 *Generally, How Do I Know If My Emotions Are Good Or Bad?*

If your emotions are absorbed in your ego, loving yourself and making yourself the centre of your world, society, and family, and wanting to take and not to give, this indicates selfish emotions. If you feel that you want to give your own self for others' progress and salvation, as Jesus Christ gave Himself for the salvation of all mankind, then these are good emotions to have.

Q7 How Can I Ensure That I Am Not A Stumbling Block Of Impure Actions Or Thoughts To Others?

We must do our best not to be stumbling blocks to others. However, sometimes even some saintly people unintentionally stumble others. As long as you are doing your best and have no bad intentions, then this is not your fault. There is no need to be upset or concerned about it, but rather pray for them.

Q8 *If You Feel That Your Ambition In Life Is To Devote All Your Time, Love, And Effort To The Lord, Then Why Do You Get Married?*

Not everyone can live unmarried. Many people are married and devote their lives to Jesus Christ. We can't say that everyone shouldn't marry, and we can't say that getting married necessarily implies that they don't devote their whole lives to Christ. There are many priests who were married and truly lived a saintly life. Father Michael Ibrahim is an example of such a person who was married and had children and performed miracles. Marriage is a holy saintly life if we are guided by the Holy Spirit.

Once, a person came up to me saying how he felt guilty because he got married. He considers it legal adultery. But this is a wrong idea. There is a difference between marriage and a lustful relationship. With lust, a person wants to satisfy their own bodily desires, and their ego is the centre. In marriage, the sexual relationship is a result, not the aim. Marriage shouldn't be the reason for satisfying one's bodily desires. Marriage is unity between two people; sexual intercourse is a result and a sign of love. It may or may not occur between a couple, such as in times of fasting, but this does not mean that they have lost their love. Love is above all things which is expressed by several means, one of which is sexual intercourse. There are some people who after having children, have lived in virginity by their own will.

They didn't feel as if they were separated but rather, they continued to love each other. The bodily intercourse does not represent an essential thing. At the same time, it's not an evil relationship. It is not forbidden, nor does it prevent us from the sanctification of life.

Q9 *You Say That God Created Everything Good. If So, Then Why Did He Allow Sin To Enter?*

God created everything good, including freedom. He sanctified the freedom of human beings. If He had prevented sin from entering the world, He is thus destroying my freedom. He does not push or encourage me to sin but on the contrary, He gives me the power to live in sanctity and holiness. I misuse freedom. Therefore, it is not God's fault but my own fault. If He prevents me from sinning, I will be like a robot or machine that has a master who directs it right or left. However, God grants us the ability to be good and to live in sanctification according to our own will, if we choose to.

Q10 What Are The Steps To Repentance?

I must discover my own weaknesses and sins. To do this requires time to examine my own soul. The problem is that if we are too involved in outside activities, we don't give our souls the opportunity to meditate under the guidance of the Holy Spirit. We need to sit by ourselves, at least once a week, to make an account of our life; our emotions, senses, activities, thoughts, time, worship, behaviour with others, faithfulness in study etc. When you know yourself, you know God. One then knows that he is a sinner and in need of the Saviour Jesus Christ. When we feel that we are above all sinners, then we are desperately in need of Jesus Christ our Redeemer. When we truly feel that we need Him, we will be able to respond to the work of the Holy Spirit in our hearts.

Two important points concerning repentance are:

1. To sit with yourself honestly and to examine your conscience through the work of the Holy Spirit within you.

2. To discover God as your Saviour, trust in Him, and ask Him to give you repentance and healing, granting you the work of the Holy Spirit in your life.

Q11 *How Can I Start To Live In Purity?*

1. Cut off all the sources of evil – bad friends, magazines, and any environmental influences that will divert you from living in purity. I must cut them off if I am serious about wanting God to work in my life. Eliminating these sources doesn't mean that I am pure, but it is a sign that I want to be God's child and in His image.

2. Give yourself time to evaluate your life and discover where you have gone wrong. Analyse your relationship with your family. For example, perhaps you are treating your parents with pride, and this is one of the serious sources of lusts. If I disobey my parents, my body will disobey my soul. This is a common problem, not only among youth but also among elders. Therefore, it is important to re-evaluate your life and your relationship with your family, your friends, church, and God.

3. Pray and ask others to pray for you – your confession father, your parents, and spiritual friends. We need to pray for each other. Start reading the Bible, repent, confess, and ask God for forgiveness.

Q12 Is The Church A Place For Sinners Or Saints?

The church is a hospital, as saint Athanasius called it, where our Saviour Jesus Christ is working for all human beings to be healed and become saints. St Paul said, 'Christ Jesus came into the world to save sinners, of whom I am chief' (1 Timothy 1:15), because he felt he needed the heavenly Physician. We never despair of anyone. When the priests and bishops were in jail at the time of President Sadat, we witnessed a violent criminal who enjoyed living there. He felt that the prison was his home and an environment wherein he could practice evil works. One day, this man came up to us and had sown his lips together with a needle. When we asked him why he had done this, he answered that it was a way through which he could cause trouble to the wardens, making it look as though they were responsible for harming him. Not only had he sown his lips together, but he had placed two knives in the door, and with his back facing the knives he cut himself and went to the priests with blood oozing out of the deep wounds. This person – who was violent even with himself – once he found love, acted like a simple child with us. Everyone needs to feel God's love working through His believers. Nobody could push or prevent such a person from doing any harm, however, love can change him. This prisoner was then serving us willingly and enjoyed being in our company.

Salvation is presented to everyone. God is waiting for everybody to return to Him and be saved. Therefore, the gates of the Church – of Paradise – are opened, waiting for all sinners without any exception, whatever sins one might have committed. The most important thing is to start to repent. The Church encourages her members to repent every day, to keep their clothes clean. Washing is continuous. Each time you pray you recite Psalm 50 (51) in the introduction of the Agpeya prayers, asking God to cleanse your soul.

Q13 ***How Can We Overcome Evil Thoughts When They Attack Us?***

We must distinguish between thoughts coming from outside and those springing forth from within us. In your age as youth, remember that you must be attacked by evil thoughts. In these circumstances, I must look at this battle as a chance to be crowned. If there is no battle, how can there be victory and how can we be crowned?! Therefore, struggle against evil thoughts and do not despair. Don't allow sin to defeat you, whatever these thoughts are, and no matter how much they attack you.

Q14 *Why Is Adultery Considered A Sin?*

You are a child of God, and God wants you to carry His image and to imitate Him. He is the Holy One. When you are deprived of holiness or sanctity of life, you deform your personality, and lose your likeness to God through acts like adultery. This is sin. Sin is not just about harming others. Think of something like adultery - when I commit adultery, I am wronging the most important being I care for... myself! I harm my purity; the divine image and likeness which God granted me. Adultery spoils this likeness to God.

Q15 How Come King David And King Solomon, Who Are Considered Men Of God, Took Many Wives To Satisfy Their Desires?

If we observe the way of life David the prophet led, we see that despite his taking many wives, he, like Abraham, did not accept these wives to satisfy his lusts. He accepted them to multiply and fill the earth. Though David had difficult experiences, he was always brave and peaceful. He had such tender feelings even towards his enemies. If he was a man of pleasure, then when he was persecuted or suffering, he would have left Israel, his people and even God. But this was not the case, for even though his life was a chain of sufferings, he never ceased praising God and singing psalms. This is most clear when he was persecuted by his son, Absalom, or by his counsellor, Ahithophel, or by his people. He wrote many psalms on these occasions and he rejoiced. Although he would start his psalms expressing his grief, he concludes by giving thanks to God. Thus, his life was free from any earthly desires. Although he fell with Uriah's wife, we shouldn't judge him as a man of pleasures as he repented for his actions with unceasing tears. If David was living just for pleasure with his wives, why didn't he struggle to take the throne? He had the chance to take it by force, but he preferred having God working in his life.

As for Solomon, he truly had a bad experience. The Holy Bible tells us that when he took his wives, especially the foreign ones, he took them for pleasure, and he had to pay the price as the book of Ecclesiasts tells us. He bore the fruit of sin, but he repented. He wrote his experiences and he gave a very good example of repentance.

But if we look at someone like Joseph, we see the great effect that purity had on his life, and indeed, the whole history of salvation.

Q16 *I Don't Like Going To Parties, But Sometimes I Have To, And I Never Feel Any Happiness. What Can I Do?*

If you do not feel happiness, why do you go?

Why do you put yourself in the way of temptation?

Now, because you are in a good spiritual condition, you don't enjoy the party. But perhaps later, even your feelings about the party may change. You must be strict and fair with yourself. When you say, 'What is wrong with dancing?' I ask you a question, 'Do you think that you are glorifying God while you are dancing?' We must speak frankly. We are the members of the body of Jesus Christ, the sons of the King of kings. We must act in a way that suits our rank. I am an ambassador sent to this world to represent my Lord Jesus Christ. Imagine if the ambassador of any state in Australia acted improperly in a way that affects the reputation of the country he represents. How would the government of his country react? It would ask him to quit. Similarly, you are the ambassador of God. You are heaven itself; whatever you do is in the name of Christ.

Q17 *I Often Have Wrong Presumptions And Wrong Suspicions, And I Know That This Is Because My Own Heart Is Impure. What Do I Do To Acquire Purity?*

As I said, we should confess our sins under the guidance of the Holy Spirit who grants us repentance, then the fruit will appear in due time. We must trust God, the Forgiver of sins, without despair nor negligence.

Once, in a visit to upper Egypt, I met with one of my confessors. He was a university student at the time, and I never saw a person so fiercely attacked by evil thoughts the way he was. He used to weep every night, saying, 'God, please release me from these impure thoughts.' He repented repeatedly but could never attain purity. So, when I met him in upper Egypt, I asked him about his life and service. He said, 'I will tell you something. These four years of struggle (at university) were advantageous for me, and for the edification of the church. When I came here to serve God in some villages, I started to work with the youth, but they were too shy to talk about their sexual problems. I used to tell them that I had the same experience, and that I often wept for my impure thoughts. They loved me because they felt I was like them. I am not a heavenly creature, but I have the same body, and the same emotions, and I was attacked by the same thoughts. In this way many of the youth repented.'

Therefore, don't be afraid of the impure thoughts, but rather struggle against them so that one day you will be pure, and you will also attract others to the life of purity.

Once, I was called to see a woman who was about forty years old, who wanted to deny Christ. She 'loved' a man who was the thirtieth of her lovers. She was staying in a hotel of bad reputation, but I felt I had to go, so I took a deacon with me who was married and went to ask for her at the hotel. She said, 'What do you want?' I said, 'I came to speak with you about our Lord Jesus Christ.' She said, 'No, I am not Christian. I don't want to speak with you. I don't love the church.' I continued speaking to her, but she was totally silent, showing no response at all. Then the deacon spoke to her, saying, 'What do you think of Abouna? Do you think that he is an angel coming down from heaven? He has the same body as yours. I myself in my youth, had a bad experience...'

She started to speak, because she felt that we were not coming to judge her, or acting as leaders, but that we were coming to participate and commune with her in Christ as the Saviour of all men. We felt her weakness as if it were our own weakness.

When we spoke with each other she said, 'What do you want, father?' I said, 'Just leave everything in the hotel and come with me.' She left everything and came to the church. Now she is married with many children and truly lives as a faithful Christian.

Therefore, don't feel troubled when you are attacked by evil thoughts, because even this experience will help you deal with the problems of the future youth when you are older, saying, 'I had the same experience, and I know how God granted me purity, and how I struggled and was serious in my life.' This does not mean driving yourself towards impurity or submitting to it! But by far, you must struggle as much as you can, and the work of God in your heart will support you.

Q18 *What Do You Mean By 'To Be Crowned' When We Experience Struggle?*

'To be crowned' means that you acknowledge you are a king or a queen in Christ (Revelation 1:6; 5:10), the King of kings (1 Timothy 6:15; Revelation 17:14) and the King of the saints (Revelation 15:3). For you have authority over your thoughts, your emotions, and your senses. As St Isaac the Hermit said, 'The Christian person is a king. He says to this thought 'Go out!' and to the other thought 'Come in'.' You feel proud that you are able to rule, not by yourself, but through God who is working in you, and this gives us a kind of satisfaction.

Q19 *What does St Paul Means In Romans 12:2 By Conforming To This World, And Being Transformed By The Renewing Of Your Mind?*

The verse reads, 'And do not be conformed to this world, but be transformed by the renewing of your mind, that you may prove what is that good and acceptable and perfect will of God'.

The world has its own form and Christ has His. You are either in the likeness of the world or the likeness of Christ. We were born in the likeness of the world through sin. But now through baptism, we are transformed and our nature is renewed. Moreover, every day through repentance, our minds are renewed by the Holy Spirit whom we have received in baptism and Chrismation. Through sin, we lost our glorious nature (our original nature), but now through baptism, we have the power to live in the likeness of our Lord Jesus Christ We must practice it through daily repentance to be transformed into the likeness of our Lord Jesus Christ.

Q20 How Can We Face The Problem Of Laziness?

This is a very simple practice that can be used not only for our spiritual struggle, but in all aspects of our lives. You must do what is important at the start, giving it the priority. For instance, when you are very tired and you want to sleep, say to yourself 'I will only pray the 'Our Father...' This takes one minute at the most, so you decide to say the 'Thanksgiving Prayer'. After this, you encourage yourself, saying that you can add Psalm 50. In this way, you will do the right thing at the right time without delay.

Don't postpone the spiritual work for tomorrow. Say, 'I will do it now and rest tomorrow.' Otherwise tomorrow will drag on to the next day etc. You will have rest when you start because the rest of the soul is more important than the comfort of the body. When I sleep with peace of mind, my body will also be comfortable, whereas if I sleep with anxiety, then even my body will feel discomfort.

Q21 ***How Can A Person Grow To Love The Life Of Prayer And Love God More?***

To love prayer, try practicing the Jesus Prayer. Repeat the words, 'My Lord, save me; my Lord forgive my sins; my Lord, have mercy on me, a sinner,' as frequently as you can all day long. Therefore, when the time of prayer comes, you will feel very comforted. But if you are occupied all day in other tasks alone without reciting these words, then when you stand to pray, you will find it difficult to contemplate on God. We need to enter an unceasing dialogue with God all day long. Then, when it's time to stand before God in prayer, we will feel comforted. It will also become a chance to judge our conscious and repent.

Q22 Is It Easy Or Hard, In This World, To Focus On My Inner Man?

It is hard if we do it trusting in our own abilities alone, but if we depend on the divine grace, sincerely struggling hard, it will be very easy.

The second element that we must consider in our spiritual struggle that we must live a communal life in Jesus Christ, caring for one another and praying for one another as well. In the book of Acts, we notice that the Apostles always lived a communal life, worshipping and working together, and struggling in the spiritual battle together. Even when St Peter was in jail, the whole church was praying in the upper room of St Mark's house (Acts 12:5,12).

When you speak to a friend over the phone, do you talk about the latest fashion or latest car, or do you speak to them about the salvation of their soul? We need a communal attitude, as well as a focus on our personal life. We cannot separate the communal life from the personal one in Jesus Christ.

Q23 *Sometimes It Is Hard To Speak To My Friends About Spiritual Thoughts. How Can I Induce These Spiritual Discussions Without Feeling Embarrassed?*

Why is it hard? Jehovah's Witnesses talk to people all the time, spreading their teachings, although they are wrong. When you speak the truth, realising the preciousness of your friend's soul, and that their success also helps your progress, then you will not be ashamed, saying to yourself, 'I am not afraid of the gospel of Christ, for it is the power of God to salvation for everyone who believes...' (Romans 1:16) Is my relationship with Christ shameful? Isn't it important to speak to your friends about the salvation of the soul, which will lead them to eternal life? Which is more shameful; a person whose conduct is sinful, or a person who wants to raise others' souls to the angelic way of life?

Sometimes, if the world cannot accept the true way in Christ, we have at least sown the seed in each person's soul and let God work. As St Paul says, 'I planted, Apollos watered, but God gave the increase.' (1 Corinthians 3:6) Maybe what I said to them will not bring forth fruits now, but maybe it will years from now. That is why it is very important to look not only to our personal life, but also our communal or group life, because as a community of Christ, we are proud to be attributed to Him and should not feel ashamed.

Q24 Sometimes It Is Easier To Tell People Who Don't Know Christ About Him Than It Is To Tell Our Family And Friends About Him. Because We Have Been Brought Up In The Traditional Church, There Are Some Who Come To Church Out Of Duty And Think They Are On The Right Track And Hence Are In Need Of No Repentance, Etc. How Do We Talk To Such People?

Youth and even children may have a strong effect on their parents, either through words or simply their behaviour. It is essential to approach our parents with wisdom, humility, and obedience, but not to forget love and gentleness.

For instance, a professor once told me that his father had said to him that when he was about eight years old, he heard in Sunday School that when we pray, God sends his angels to protect us. He went home that day and noticed his dad going to sleep without praying so he said to him, 'Father, how can you sleep without praying? Don't you want the angel of God to protect you?' His father told his son that from that day on he never slept without praying.

We must work wisely, obediently, and kindly, without despair, because every seed will surely bear fruits. However, do not consider yourself as a teacher to your parents, but rather deal with them through love.

Q25 *Is It Enough To Be Pure Inside And Have Good Intentions, Saying The Holy Spirit Is Filling My Heart And Guiding Me, And To Ignore Fasting, Reading The Bible Or Going To Church?*

In our Orthodox faith, we never separate the inner life from the outer life, or the work of the soul from the work of the body. When we are fasting, this helps our prayer become more spiritual. Therefore, the body participates with the soul in its spiritual struggle, as it does when we pray standing up. Those who truly and sincerely read the Bible have purity not only in their hearts, but also in their bodies. Therefore, we do not want to separate the inner life from practicing worship in our outer life.

Q26 ***If You Feel That You Are Close To God, But You Have Something Upsetting You From God, What Can You Do If You Get No Answer To Your Prayers And Your Problem Remains Unsolved?***

A person's life can never be free from problems – every day we face new problems. If at times we can't bear the burden, we can express our upset to God and ask Him 'why are you hiding Your Face, O Lord!' Speak frankly with your God, for you have no one else to seek but Him.

Tell Him, 'Truly You are the Creator, and I am Your creation, but I want to discover Your mysteries. Grant me faith that You are always working for the good, even if I am in a difficult situation.'

Q27 How Can We Keep Our Friendships And Relationships Pure, Especially With Friends From The Opposite Sex?

They are not the opposite sex, but rather the other sex, for they are on the same path with us. Our Lord Jesus Christ said, 'I am the way,' for both sexes. When I am among friends, I should keep my relationship pure.

We must ask ourselves a few questions and observe some points:

a) When I form a friendship with someone, is Jesus Christ a partner in this relationship? In other words, is He blessing it? Am I growing in grace and faith, or am I losing my way because of bad company? As our early fathers expressed – if you are in good company, your spiritual life will progress, and if you are in bad company, you are liable to fall or at least step backward.

b) If you feel like hiding your acts, beware, for you are doing wrong. Be honest with yourself, frank with your parents, confession father and first and foremost with God.

c) Don't always stay with the same friend. You must ask yourself about the aim of this friendship; whether it is to glorify God or not. Being with different friends is a chance to acquire good things from different people, as the bee that picks good nectar from every flower.

d) You must regard your friend as if they are your sister or brother. Would you accept your sister having an impure relationship with another boy? Here is a real story that I think answers my question.

Last summer, a person came to me upset about the priests in Alexandria, for they wouldn't allow him to carry on his friendship with some girlfriends. He said to me, 'If you are my confession father, will you allow me to have these friendships?' I smiled and said, 'I want you to speak to me openly and frankly.' He started speaking about the first girlfriend, saying she was spiritual and liked the church, loved God, etc... I asked him, 'And what is the outcome of this relationship?' He said, 'I hope that I can marry her.' So, I told him to speak with her father and mother, so that both families know, and she must speak frankly with her confession father. Then he started to speak about the second girl. He praised her, and at the end he had forgotten what he had already said about the first one, and I asked, 'What is the outcome of this relationship?' He said, 'I hope that I will marry her.' I did not comment until the end, and he spoke the same way about a third girl. He simply wanted to satisfy his own emotions under the name of love, deceiving himself

Therefore, we must speak openly to our parents, confession father, and primarily with God.

Thus, you will have the answer as to whether this is a healthy friendship or not. Don't expect anyone else to answer the question for you, because you know what is good for your spiritual progress and what would be a disadvantage for you.

Q28 In 2 Corinthians 7:1, St Paul Talks About Filthiness Of The Flesh And Spirit. What Does He Mean?

The filthiness of the flesh is bodily lusts, greed etc. The spirit's filthiness is pride, vainglory etc. There are spiritual faults of the soul, and bodily sins of the flesh.

Q29 *What Is Wrong With Thoughts if I Don't Harm Anyone By Them?*

Our minds are God's creation, and we should keep them holy by permitting only pure thoughts.

Beware of evil thoughts that Satan introduces, for they ruin you. When evil thoughts attack you, don't allow them in, but say, 'Christ is my Lord who reigns in my mind, that my thoughts may be pure and holy, with no trace of impurity.'

We have a heavenly mind over which God reigns. Our minds are a dwelling place for God, who sanctifies everything: our bodies, minds, emotions, and senses, but this doesn't mean we become isolated from society. For Jesus Christ Himself is pure and was living in the society. We see Him through our senses and emotions.

God's aim is to sanctify our emotions, to love God and men. This enables us to express our emotions, sharing sorrow with the suffering, and joy with the elated. God is readily willing to guide our emotions in the right way if we ask Him seriously.

Q30 It Is Difficult Talking To My Parents Because We Always Fight.

It is important that you converse with your parents in love, speaking in a gentle and calm manner. St Dorotheos stated that our relationship with our parents or any person looks like a circle, and its centre is God. If I walk towards God, surely, I will be close to my mum and dad, my friends and even my enemies. If I live in Him, I will be able to attract others to God, even those who are in enmity with me.

First, we should reconcile with God, and once we draw closer to Him, then we can draw closer to each other. That is, one should have peace with God and with themselves through repentance, and this leads to reconciliation with others – even with enemies. The further away I am from God, the further away from others (including my parents) I will be.

Q31 *Why Is using Foul Language Wrong?*

It is important to behave in a decent and pleasant way, even towards those who insult us or tease us. Foul language contradicts the Christian ideas of peace, love, and kindness. Using these tools, you can attract others to the right Christian attitude.

Q32 *I Find It Difficult Talking To My Parents Without Getting Into An Argument.*

It is important for you to choose the suitable time, method, and words to communicate with your parents. If you are wise and gentle, you will be able to communicate and discuss issues with them. You can help them understand your perspective by your pure Christian life and faith, and they will be able to talk to you in a gentle manner. It is important that you correct your own life first before criticising the life of others.

Try to be understanding and logical, and don't consider yourself right all the time – we all have our faults! On the other hand, your parents must have something good. Don't refuse everything they say just because they might be old fashioned – reconsider this, and it will be for your edification.

Q33 *If You Say A Word Which Harms A Person Unintentionally, Is It A Sin?*

Don't look to any action or deed as being a sin or not. You are God's child, and you should consider every soul as something precious in your eyes.

If I feel someone has misunderstood my comment, I contact him and apologise. Your sole aim is to edify others and bring them closer to God.

Q34 *What Advice Would You Give To A Young Man Who Is In Love With A Girl, And Who Is Unable To Free Himself From That Love?*

Undoubtedly, falling in love is not an easy situation to free oneself from, especially for a relationship which lasted for a long time. However, we know of many young men who managed, through the grace of God, to sever a relationship unequivocally. The remnants of those relationships were external struggles waged against Satan-induced thoughts or dreams, reminding the person of past exploits, or attempting to revive within him dormant desires. What, then, is the path to victory? The path is summarised in the answer to the next question.

Q35 Given That Love Is An Emotion, Would Willpower Have A Role, Or Would Love Dominate?

a) We must have faith that through the grace of God, we will be able to liberate ourselves, however strong the feelings, ties and emotions may be.

b) We have been created as beings with intelligence. An animal behaves fully in accordance with its instincts, not being endowed with the willpower to challenge the course of nature. But you, a human being, are capable of changing instinct's course, despite its strong influence, removing its effect on your behaviour.

You might argue that, practically, you are unable to apply this theoretical viewpoint. I would counter that even though you might have willingly accepted to be enslaved as such, you still have the Lord's Cross (the power of God) through which sin is demolished, and with which your love and instincts are purified.

c) For this reason, and for the Lord to liberate you, you should fast and pray ardently crying, 'My Lord make me repent; render sin bitter in my mouth!'

d) It is necessary to find a substitute. You love this girl because she is pretty, or well-dressed, or witty; how can you rid yourself of this infatuation? Contemplate the Lord's beauty and majesty, His gentleness and fatherly tenderness, and His bounties and blessings to you. Love the One hanging on the Cross.

e) Be very strict with yourself; do not pamper your soul. If it is not drawn to Christ's love, contemplate death, and remember the awesome Judgment Day, and the fact that you are accountable for each word, deed, or unclean thought.

f) Remember who you are. You are God's creation. Your body is the Lord's. You carry the status of child of God. Your place is in the bosom of God. Repeat all day long, 'Is it befitting for a child of God to think in this way?'

g) Be candid with your father in confession. Talk to him; he is your father, your guide, and your physician. Be open with him since sin abhors light and thrives in darkness. The longer you hide it, awaiting more favourable circumstances for your confession, the stronger its grasp on you.

h) As far as practicable, sever your relationship completely with the girl, and do not allow your thoughts to wander back to her.

Q36 *Is There Any Danger Associated With A Young Man Meeting A Young Lady Among Church Goers, If He Happens To Have Been Deprived From His Deceased Mother's Love?*

The girl's presence in church does not necessarily mean that she does not err, or that she has lost her femininity. If you need sympathy for the loss of your mother and her tenderness, then seeking a girl to make up for this loss carries three hazards:

a) Your expectation of the girl's sympathy or tenderness stems from selfishness on your part and, if offered to the girl, will be mixed with physical tendencies.

b) Such a pursuit risks eroding your personality. You, as a child of God, should not beg pity from another human being. Our Lord Jesus, your God, is capable of flooding you with His love. You can challenge the desire to fill this void from other people, instead of Christ, by channelling your energy into work and struggle. Take the example of many famous inventors lost their parents early in life who emerged in triumph not humiliation. Indeed, look to Christ, who already envelops you with an amazing love. You only need to open the eyes of your heart to appreciate His tenderness towards you.

c) What is the goal or outcome of such a relationship? After marrying this girl, do you expect her to fulfill the functions of a mother? Or would you not want that relationship to be based on love exchanged in Christ Jesus?

Q37 *Despite Me Having Loved Everyone Indiscriminately, A Young Lady Is Attracted To Me, And I Am Not Sure What To Do, Especially As She Is A Devout Christian.*

How did you conclude that the girl is a devout Christian? It is likely that her attraction to you reflects a weakness in her life which needs rectification, not the other way around. If you really loved her in Christ, flee from her, for your salvation and for hers. Finally, bear in mind that Satan tempted Christ on the temple's pinnacle; there is nothing stopping him from working here, taking advantage of her circumstances. This is likely, even if she were a servant in church, and even if everyone were to testify to her piousness.

It should be noted, though, that we are neither promoting full isolation from society, nor are we equating instincts with sin. Rather, the arguments presented above are directed to the person who feels a particular attraction towards a certain person of the other sex. This is the relationship which requires complete severance. May the Lord grant that His grace work within us and sanctify us unto the end. Amen.

Scan the QR code to go to our website where you will find

- Book reviews
- Great deals
- Our full library of books

www.ingramcontent.com/pod-product-compliance
Lightning Source LLC
LaVergne TN
LVHW051009080826
845145LV00009B/2534